I0188041

This planner belongs to:

Also by Sze Wing Vetault:

<u>Books and Planners</u>

Goddess with Many Faces

21 Days of Inspiration

Goddess Planner 2021

Goddess Planner (Undated)

Goddess Daily Planner

For more information, please visit:
www.SzeWingVetault.com

This Goddess Daily Planner is created by Sze Wing Vetault
Copyright© 2021 by Sze Wing Vetault. All rights reserved.

"Without leaps of imagination or dreaming, we lose the excitement of possibilities. Dreaming, after all, is a form of planning."
– Gloria Steinem

I hope this Goddess Daily Planner will serve you both, dreaming and planning.

With love,

Sze Wing Vetault

Plan My Day

DATE:

This morning I feel ...

Fine

Tired   Good

Exhasuted   Fantastic

I feel this way because...

To feel more energized & inspired
I can ...

Today my top 3 priority actions are:

Dreams/First thoughts

Reminders/Appointments

Brain Dump/Reminder/Notes

AM

PM

Today, I am grateful for ......
and I appreciate ......

Plan My Day

DATE:

This morning I feel ...

Fine

Tired   Good

Exhasuted   Fantastic

I feel this way because...

To feel more energized & inspired
I can ...

Today my top 3 priority actions are:

Dreams/First thoughts

Reminders/Appointments

AM

PM

Brain Dump/Reminder/Notes

Today, I am grateful for ......
and I appreciate ......

Plan My Day

DATE:

This morning I feel ...

Fine
Tired   Good
Exhasuted   Fantastic

I feel this way because...

To feel more energized & inspired
I can ...

Today my top 3 priority actions are:

Dreams/First thoughts

Reminders/Appointments

AM

PM

Brain Dump/Reminder/Notes

Today, I am grateful for ......
and I appreciate ......

Plan My Day

DATE:

This morning I feel ...

Fine

Tired   Good

Exhasuted   Fantastic

I feel this way because...

Today my top 3 priority actions are:

To feel more energized & inspired
I can ...

Dreams/First thoughts

Reminders/Appointments

AM

PM

Brain Dump/Reminder/Notes

Today, I am grateful for ......
and I appreciate ......

Plan My Day

DATE:

This morning I feel ...

Fine
Tired   Good
Exhasuted   Fantastic

I feel this way because...

Today my top 3 priority actions are:

To feel more energized & inspired
I can ...

Dreams/First thoughts

Reminders/Appointments

AM

PM

Brain Dump/Reminder/Notes

Today, I am grateful for ......
and I appreciate ......

Plan My Day

DATE:

This morning I feel ...

Today my top 3 priority actions are:

Fine

Tired   Good

Exhasuted   Fantastic

I feel this way because...

To feel more energized & inspired
I can ...

Dreams/First thoughts

Reminders/Appointments

Brain Dump/Reminder/Notes

AM

PM

Today, I am grateful for ......
and I appreciate ......

Self-Reflection

Colouring Mandala

Plan My Day

DATE:

This morning I feel ...

Fine

Tired   Good

Exhasuted   Fantastic

I feel this way because...

Today my top 3 priority actions are:

To feel more energized & inspired
I can ...

Dreams/First thoughts

Reminders/Appointments

AM

_____

_____

_____

_____

_____

PM

_____

_____

_____

_____

_____

Brain Dump/Reminder/Notes

Today, I am grateful for ......
and I appreciate ......

Plan My Day

DATE:

This morning I feel ...

Fine

Tired   Good

Exhasuted   Fantastic

I feel this way because...

To feel more energized & inspired
I can ...

Reminders/Appointments

AM

PM

Today my top 3 priority actions are:

Dreams/First thoughts

Brain Dump/Reminder/Notes

Today, I am grateful for ......
and I appreciate ......

Plan My Day

DATE:

This morning I feel ...

Fine

Tired　　　Good

Exhasuted　　　Fantastic

I feel this way because...

Today my top 3 priority actions are:

To feel more energized & inspired
I can ...

Dreams/First thoughts

Reminders/Appointments

AM

PM

Brain Dump/Reminder/Notes

Today, I am grateful for ......
and I appreciate ......

Plan My Day

DATE:

This morning I feel ...

Fine

Tired   Good

Exhasuted   Fantastic

I feel this way because...

Today my top 3 priority actions are:

To feel more energized & inspired I can ...

Dreams/First thoughts

Reminders/Appointments

AM

Brain Dump/Reminder/Notes

PM

Today, I am grateful for ......
and I appreciate ......

Plan My Day

DATE:

This morning I feel ...

Today my top 3 priority actions are:

Fine

Tired   Good

Exhasuted   Fantastic

I feel this way because...

To feel more energized & inspired
I can ...

Dreams/First thoughts

Reminders/Appointments

Brain Dump/Reminder/Notes

AM

PM

Today, I am grateful for ......
and I appreciate ......

Plan My Day

DATE:

This morning I feel ...

Fine

Tired   Good

Exhasuted   Fantastic

I feel this way because...

To feel more energized & inspired
I can ...

Reminders/Appointments

AM

PM

Today my top 3 priority actions are:

Dreams/First thoughts

Brain Dump/Reminder/Notes

Today, I am grateful for ......
and I appreciate ......

Self-Reflection

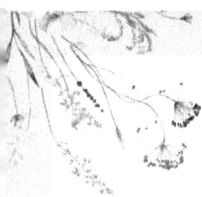

Just Doodle

dream

Plan My Day

DATE:

This morning I feel ...

Fine

Tired   Good

Exhasuted   Fantastic

I feel this way because...

Today my top 3 priority actions are:

To feel more energized & inspired
I can ...

Dreams/First thoughts

Reminders/Appointments

Brain Dump/Reminder/Notes

AM

PM

Today, I am grateful for ......
and I appreciate ......

Plan My Day

DATE:

This morning I feel ...

Fine

Tired   Good

Exhasuted   Fantastic

I feel this way because...

Today my top 3 priority actions are:

To feel more energized & inspired
I can ...

Dreams/First thoughts

Reminders/Appointments

AM

PM

Brain Dump/Reminder/Notes

Today, I am grateful for ......
and I appreciate ......

Plan My Day

DATE:

This morning I feel ...

Fine

Tired   Good

Exhasuted   Fantastic

I feel this way because...

Today my top 3 priority actions are:

To feel more energized & inspired
I can ...

Dreams/First thoughts

Reminders/Appointments

Brain Dump/Reminder/Notes

AM

PM

Today, I am grateful for ......
and I appreciate ......

Plan My Day

DATE:

This morning I feel ...

Fine

Tired   Good

Exhasuted   Fantastic

I feel this way because...

Today my top 3 priority actions are:

To feel more energized & inspired
I can ...

Dreams/First thoughts

Reminders/Appointments

AM

PM

Brain Dump/Reminder/Notes

Today, I am grateful for ......
and I appreciate ......

Plan My Day

DATE:

This morning I feel ...

Fine

Tired

Good

Exhasuted

Fantastic

I feel this way because...

Today my top 3 priority actions are:

To feel more energized & inspired
I can ...

Dreams/First thoughts

Reminders/Appointments

Brain Dump/Reminder/Notes

AM

PM

Today, I am grateful for ......
and I appreciate ......

Plan My Day

DATE:

This morning I feel ...

Fine
Tired   Good
Exhasuted   Fantastic

I feel this way because...

To feel more energized & inspired
I can ...

Today my top 3 priority actions are:

Dreams/First thoughts

Reminders/Appointments

AM

PM

Brain Dump/Reminder/Notes

Today, I am grateful for ......
and I appreciate ......

Self-Reflection

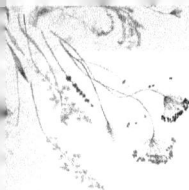

Turning It Over

My To-Do List

Universe To-Do List

Plan My Day

DATE:

This morning I feel ...

Fine

Tired　　　　　Good

Exhasuted　　　　Fantastic

I feel this way because...

Today my top 3 priority actions are:

To feel more energized & inspired
I can ...

Dreams/First thoughts

Reminders/Appointments

Brain Dump/Reminder/Notes

AM

PM

Today, I am grateful for ......
and I appreciate ......

Plan My Day

DATE:

This morning I feel ...

Fine

Tired   Good

Exhasuted   Fantastic

I feel this way because...

Today my top 3 priority actions are:

To feel more energized & inspired
I can ...

Dreams/First thoughts

Reminders/Appointments

Brain Dump/Reminder/Notes

AM

PM

Today, I am grateful for ......
and I appreciate ......

Plan My Day

DATE:

This morning I feel ...

Fine

Tired   Good

Exhasuted   Fantastic

I feel this way because...

**To feel more energized & inspired
I can ...**

Today my top 3 priority actions are:

Dreams/First thoughts

Reminders/Appointments

AM

PM

Brain Dump/Reminder/Notes

Today, I am grateful for ......
and I appreciate ......

Plan My Day

DATE:

This morning I feel ...

Fine

Tired   Good

Exhasuted   Fantastic

I feel this way because...

Today my top 3 priority actions are:

To feel more energized & inspired
I can ...

Dreams/First thoughts

Reminders/Appointments

Brain Dump/Reminder/Notes

AM

PM

Today, I am grateful for ......
and I appreciate ......

Plan My Day

DATE:

This morning I feel ...

Fine

Tired   Good

Exhasuted   Fantastic

I feel this way because...

Today my top 3 priority actions are:

To feel more energized & inspired
I can ...

Dreams/First thoughts

Reminders/Appointments

AM

PM

Brain Dump/Reminder/Notes

Today, I am grateful for ......
and I appreciate ......

Plan My Day

DATE:

This morning I feel ...

Fine

Tired   Good

Exhasuted   Fantastic

I feel this way because...

Today my top 3 priority actions are:

To feel more energized & inspired
I can ...

Dreams/First thoughts

Reminders/Appointments

Brain Dump/Reminder/Notes

AM

PM

Today, I am grateful for ......
and I appreciate ......

Self-Reflection

Complete the Maze

Plan My Day

DATE:

This morning I feel ...

Fine

Tired   Good

Exhasuted   Fantastic

I feel this way because...

To feel more energized & inspired
I can ...

Today my top 3 priority actions are:

Dreams/First thoughts

Reminders/Appointments

AM

PM

Brain Dump/Reminder/Notes

Today, I am grateful for ......
and I appreciate ......

Plan My Day

DATE:

This morning I feel ...

Fine

Tired   Good

Exhasuted   Fantastic

I feel this way because...

Today my top 3 priority actions are:

To feel more energized & inspired
I can ...

Dreams/First thoughts

Reminders/Appointments

Brain Dump/Reminder/Notes

AM

PM

Today, I am grateful for ......
and I appreciate ......

Plan My Day

DATE:

This morning I feel ...

Fine

Tired   Good

Exhasuted   Fantastic

I feel this way because...

Today my top 3 priority actions are:

To feel more energized & inspired
I can ...

Dreams/First thoughts

Reminders/Appointments

AM

PM

Brain Dump/Reminder/Notes

Today, I am grateful for ......
and I appreciate ......

Plan My Day

DATE:

This morning I feel ...

Fine
Tired   Good
Exhasuted   Fantastic

I feel this way because...

Today my top 3 priority actions are:

To feel more energized & inspired
I can ...

Dreams/First thoughts

Reminders/Appointments

AM

PM

Brain Dump/Reminder/Notes

Today, I am grateful for ......
and I appreciate ......

Plan My Day

DATE:

This morning I feel ...

Fine
Tired   Good
Exhasuted   Fantastic

I feel this way because...

Today my top 3 priority actions are:

To feel more energized & inspired
I can ...

Dreams/First thoughts

Reminders/Appointments

AM

PM

Brain Dump/Reminder/Notes

Today, I am grateful for ......
and I appreciate ......

Plan My Day

DATE:

This morning I feel ...

Fine

Tired   Good

Exhasuted   Fantastic

I feel this way because...

To feel more energized & inspired
I can ...

Reminders/Appointments

AM

PM

Today my top 3 priority actions are:

Dreams/First thoughts

Brain Dump/Reminder/Notes

Today, I am grateful for ......
and I appreciate ......

Self-Reflection

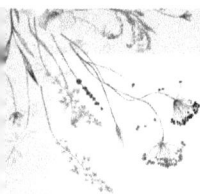

Colouring Chakra

Plan My Day

DATE:

This morning I feel ...

Fine

Tired   Good

Exhasuted   Fantastic

I feel this way because...

To feel more energized & inspired
I can ...

Today my top 3 priority actions are:

Dreams/First thoughts

Reminders/Appointments

AM

PM

Brain Dump/Reminder/Notes

Today, I am grateful for ......
and I appreciate ......

Plan My Day

DATE:

This morning I feel ...

Fine

Tired   Good

Exhasuted   Fantastic

I feel this way because...

Today my top 3 priority actions are:

To feel more energized & inspired
I can ...

Dreams/First thoughts

Reminders/Appointments

AM

PM

Brain Dump/Reminder/Notes

Today, I am grateful for ......
and I appreciate ......

Plan My Day

DATE:

This morning I feel ...

Fine

Tired   Good

Exhasuted   Fantastic

I feel this way because...

Today my top 3 priority actions are:

To feel more energized & inspired
I can ...

Dreams/First thoughts

Reminders/Appointments

AM

PM

Brain Dump/Reminder/Notes

Today, I am grateful for ......
and I appreciate ......

Plan My Day

DATE:

This morning I feel ...

Fine

Tired   Good

Exhasuted   Fantastic

I feel this way because...

Today my top 3 priority actions are:

To feel more energized & inspired
I can ...

Dreams/First thoughts

Reminders/Appointments

AM

PM

Brain Dump/Reminder/Notes

Today, I am grateful for ......
and I appreciate ......

Plan My Day

DATE:

This morning I feel ...

Fine

Tired   Good

Exhasuted   Fantastic

I feel this way because...

Today my top 3 priority actions are:

To feel more energized & inspired
I can ...

Dreams/First thoughts

Reminders/Appointments

AM

PM

Brain Dump/Reminder/Notes

Today, I am grateful for ......
and I appreciate ......

Plan My Day

DATE:

This morning I feel ...

Fine

Tired   Good

Exhasuted   Fantastic

I feel this way because...

To feel more energized & inspired
I can ...

Reminders/Appointments

AM

PM

Today my top 3 priority actions are:

Dreams/First thoughts

Brain Dump/Reminder/Notes

Today, I am grateful for ......
and I appreciate ......

Self-Reflection

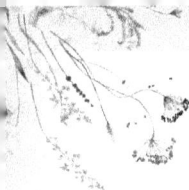

Complete the Sentences

I like...

I wish ...

I wonder ...

Plan My Day

DATE:

This morning I feel ...

Fine
Tired   Good
Exhasuted   Fantastic

I feel this way because...

To feel more energized & inspired
I can ...

Today my top 3 priority actions are:

Dreams/First thoughts

Reminders/Appointments

AM

PM

Brain Dump/Reminder/Notes

Today, I am grateful for ......
and I appreciate ......

Plan My Day

DATE:

This morning I feel ...

Fine

Tired   Good

Exhasuted   Fantastic

I feel this way because...

Today my top 3 priority actions are:

To feel more energized & inspired
I can ...

Dreams/First thoughts

Reminders/Appointments

Brain Dump/Reminder/Notes

AM

PM

Today, I am grateful for ......
and I appreciate ......

Plan My Day

DATE:

This morning I feel ...

Fine

Tired   Good

Exhasuted   Fantastic

I feel this way because...

Today my top 3 priority actions are:

To feel more energized & inspired
I can ...

Dreams/First thoughts

Reminders/Appointments

AM

PM

Brain Dump/Reminder/Notes

Today, I am grateful for ......
and I appreciate ......

Plan My Day

DATE:

This morning I feel ...

Fine

Tired   Good

Exhasuted   Fantastic

I feel this way because...

Today my top 3 priority actions are:

To feel more energized & inspired
I can ...

Dreams/First thoughts

Reminders/Appointments

AM

PM

Brain Dump/Reminder/Notes

Today, I am grateful for ......
and I appreciate ......

Plan My Day

DATE: _____

This morning I feel ...

Fine

Tired   Good

Exhasuted   Fantastic

I feel this way because...

Today my top 3 priority actions are:

To feel more energized & inspired
I can ...

Dreams/First thoughts

Reminders/Appointments

AM
_____
_____
_____
_____
_____

PM
_____
_____
_____
_____
_____
_____

Brain Dump/Reminder/Notes

Today, I am grateful for ......
and I appreciate ......

Plan My Day

DATE:

This morning I feel ...

Fine

Tired   Good

Exhasuted   Fantastic

I feel this way because...

Today my top 3 priority actions are:

To feel more energized & inspired
I can ...

Dreams/First thoughts

Reminders/Appointments

AM

PM

Brain Dump/Reminder/Notes

Today, I am grateful for ......
and I appreciate ......

Self-Reflection

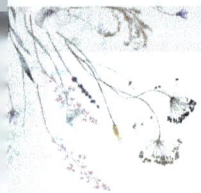

Just Doodle

Plan My Day

DATE:

This morning I feel ...

Fine

Tired   Good

Exhasuted   Fantastic

I feel this way because...

Today my top 3 priority actions are:

To feel more energized & inspired
I can ...

Dreams/First thoughts

Reminders/Appointments

AM

PM

Brain Dump/Reminder/Notes

Today, I am grateful for ......
and I appreciate ......

Plan My Day

DATE:

This morning I feel ...

Fine

Tired   Good

Exhasuted   Fantastic

I feel this way because...

Today my top 3 priority actions are:

To feel more energized & inspired
I can ...

Dreams/First thoughts

Reminders/Appointments

Brain Dump/Reminder/Notes

AM

PM

Today, I am grateful for ......
and I appreciate ......

Plan My Day

DATE:

This morning I feel ...

Fine

Tired   Good

Exhasuted   Fantastic

I feel this way because...

Today my top 3 priority actions are:

To feel more energized & inspired
I can ...

Dreams/First thoughts

Reminders/Appointments

AM

PM

Brain Dump/Reminder/Notes

Today, I am grateful for ......
and I appreciate ......

Plan My Day

DATE:

This morning I feel ...

Fine

Tired   Good

Exhasuted   Fantastic

I feel this way because...

Today my top 3 priority actions are:

To feel more energized & inspired
I can ...

Dreams/First thoughts

Reminders/Appointments

AM

PM

Brain Dump/Reminder/Notes

Today, I am grateful for ......
and I appreciate ......

Plan My Day

DATE:

This morning I feel ...

Fine

Tired   Good

Exhasuted   Fantastic

I feel this way because...

Today my top 3 priority actions are:

To feel more energized & inspired
I can ...

Dreams/First thoughts

Reminders/Appointments

AM

PM

Brain Dump/Reminder/Notes

Today, I am grateful for ......
and I appreciate ......

Plan My Day

DATE:

This morning I feel ...

Fine

Tired   Good

Exhasuted   Fantastic

I feel this way because...

Today my top 3 priority actions are:

To feel more energized & inspired
I can ...

Dreams/First thoughts

Reminders/Appointments

Brain Dump/Reminder/Notes

AM

PM

Today, I am grateful for ......
and I appreciate ......

Self-Reflection

Complete the Picture

"Happy as a clam"

Plan My Day

DATE:

This morning I feel ...

Fine

Tired   Good

Exhasuted   Fantastic

I feel this way because...

Today my top 3 priority actions are:

To feel more energized & inspired
I can ...

Dreams/First thoughts

Reminders/Appointments

AM

PM

Brain Dump/Reminder/Notes

Today, I am grateful for ......
and I appreciate ......

Plan My Day

DATE:

This morning I feel ...

Fine

Tired   Good

Exhasuted   Fantastic

I feel this way because...

Today my top 3 priority actions are:

To feel more energized & inspired
I can ...

Dreams/First thoughts

Reminders/Appointments

AM

PM

Brain Dump/Reminder/Notes

Today, I am grateful for ......
and I appreciate ......

Plan My Day

DATE:

This morning I feel ...

Fine

Tired   Good

Exhasuted   Fantastic

I feel this way because...

Today my top 3 priority actions are:

To feel more energized & inspired
I can ...

Dreams/First thoughts

Reminders/Appointments

Brain Dump/Reminder/Notes

AM

PM

Today, I am grateful for ......
and I appreciate ......

Plan My Day

DATE:

This morning I feel ...

Fine

Tired

Good

Exhasuted

Fantastic

I feel this way because...

Today my top 3 priority actions are:

To feel more energized & inspired
I can ...

Dreams/First thoughts

Reminders/Appointments

AM

PM

Brain Dump/Reminder/Notes

Today, I am grateful for ......
and I appreciate ......

Plan My Day

DATE:

This morning I feel ...

Fine

Tired   Good

Exhasuted   Fantastic

I feel this way because...

To feel more energized & inspired
I can ...

Today my top 3 priority actions are:

Dreams/First thoughts

Reminders/Appointments

AM

PM

Brain Dump/Reminder/Notes

Today, I am grateful for ......
and I appreciate ......

Plan My Day

DATE:

This morning I feel ...

Fine

Tired   Good

Exhasuted   Fantastic

I feel this way because...

Today my top 3 priority actions are:

To feel more energized & inspired
I can ...

Dreams/First thoughts

Reminders/Appointments

AM

PM

Brain Dump/Reminder/Notes

Today, I am grateful for ......
and I appreciate ......

Self-Reflection

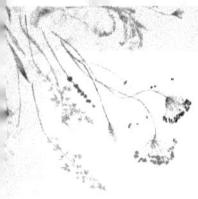

Complete the Sentences

Wouldn't it be nice if ...

Wouldn't it be nice if ...

Wouldn't it be nice if ...

Plan My Day

DATE:

This morning I feel ...

Fine

Tired   Good

Exhasuted   Fantastic

I feel this way because...

Today my top 3 priority actions are:

To feel more energized & inspired
I can ...

Dreams/First thoughts

Reminders/Appointments

AM

PM

Brain Dump/Reminder/Notes

Today, I am grateful for ......
and I appreciate ......

Plan My Day

DATE:

This morning I feel ...

Fine

Tired   Good

Exhasuted   Fantastic

I feel this way because...

Today my top 3 priority actions are:

To feel more energized & inspired
I can ...

Dreams/First thoughts

Reminders/Appointments

Brain Dump/Reminder/Notes

AM

PM

Today, I am grateful for ......
and I appreciate ......

Plan My Day

DATE:

This morning I feel ...

Fine

Tired   Good

Exhasuted   Fantastic

I feel this way because...

Today my top 3 priority actions are:

To feel more energized & inspired
I can ...

Dreams/First thoughts

Reminders/Appointments

Brain Dump/Reminder/Notes

AM

PM

Today, I am grateful for ......
and I appreciate ......

Plan My Day

DATE:

This morning I feel ...

Fine

Tired   Good

Exhasuted   Fantastic

I feel this way because...

Today my top 3 priority actions are:

To feel more energized & inspired
I can ...

Dreams/First thoughts

Reminders/Appointments

AM

PM

Brain Dump/Reminder/Notes

Today, I am grateful for ......
and I appreciate ......

Plan My Day

DATE:

This morning I feel ...

Fine

Tired   Good

Exhasuted   Fantastic

I feel this way because...

Today my top 3 priority actions are:

To feel more energized & inspired
I can ...

Dreams/First thoughts

Reminders/Appointments

AM

PM

Brain Dump/Reminder/Notes

Today, I am grateful for ......
and I appreciate ......

Plan My Day

DATE:

This morning I feel ...

Fine

Tired   Good

Exhasuted   Fantastic

I feel this way because...

Today my top 3 priority actions are:

To feel more energized & inspired
I can ...

Dreams/First thoughts

Reminders/Appointments

Brain Dump/Reminder/Notes

AM

PM

Today, I am grateful for ......
and I appreciate ......

Self-Reflection

Colouring Mandala

Plan My Day

DATE:

This morning I feel ...

Fine

Tired   Good

Exhasuted   Fantastic

I feel this way because...

Today my top 3 priority actions are:

To feel more energized & inspired
I can ...

Dreams/First thoughts

Reminders/Appointments

AM

PM

Brain Dump/Reminder/Notes

Today, I am grateful for ......
and I appreciate ......

Plan My Day

DATE:

This morning I feel ...

Fine

Tired   Good

Exhasuted   Fantastic

I feel this way because...

Today my top 3 priority actions are:

To feel more energized & inspired
I can ...

Dreams/First thoughts

Reminders/Appointments

AM

PM

Brain Dump/Reminder/Notes

Today, I am grateful for ......
and I appreciate ......

Plan My Day

This morning I feel ...

Fine

Tired   Good

Exhasuted   Fantastic

I feel this way because...

Today my top 3 priority actions are:

To feel more energized & inspired
I can ...

Dreams/First thoughts

Reminders/Appointments

Brain Dump/Reminder/Notes

AM

PM

Today, I am grateful for ......
and I appreciate ......

Plan My Day

DATE:

This morning I feel ...

Fine

Tired   Good

Exhasuted   Fantastic

I feel this way because...

Today my top 3 priority actions are:

To feel more energized & inspired
I can ...

Dreams/First thoughts

Reminders/Appointments

Brain Dump/Reminder/Notes

AM

PM

Today, I am grateful for ......
and I appreciate ......

Plan My Day

DATE:

This morning I feel …

Fine
Tired   Good
Exhasuted   Fantastic

I feel this way because…

Today my top 3 priority actions are:

To feel more energized & inspired
I can …

Dreams/First thoughts

Reminders/Appointments

Brain Dump/Reminder/Notes

AM

PM

Today, I am grateful for ……
and I appreciate ……

Plan My Day

DATE:

This morning I feel ...

Fine

Tired   Good

Exhasuted   Fantastic

I feel this way because...

Today my top 3 priority actions are:

To feel more energized & inspired
I can ...

Dreams/First thoughts

Reminders/Appointments

AM

PM

Brain Dump/Reminder/Notes

Today, I am grateful for ......
and I appreciate ......

Self-Reflection

Just Doodle

Plan My Day

DATE:

This morning I feel ...

Fine
Tired   Good
Exhasuted   Fantastic

I feel this way because...

Today my top 3 priority actions are:

To feel more energized & inspired
I can ...

Dreams/First thoughts

Reminders/Appointments

AM

PM

Brain Dump/Reminder/Notes

Today, I am grateful for ......
and I appreciate ......

Plan My Day

DATE:

This morning I feel ...

Fine

Tired   Good

Exhasuted   Fantastic

I feel this way because...

Today my top 3 priority actions are:

To feel more energized & inspired
I can ...

Dreams/First thoughts

Reminders/Appointments

Brain Dump/Reminder/Notes

AM

PM

Today, I am grateful for ......
and I appreciate ......

Plan My Day

DATE:

This morning I feel ...

Fine

Tired   Good

Exhasuted   Fantastic

I feel this way because...

Today my top 3 priority actions are:

To feel more energized & inspired
I can ...

Dreams/First thoughts

Reminders/Appointments

Brain Dump/Reminder/Notes

AM

PM

Today, I am grateful for ......
and I appreciate ......

Plan My Day

DATE:

This morning I feel ...

Fine

Tired   Good

Exhasuted   Fantastic

I feel this way because...

Today my top 3 priority actions are:

To feel more energized & inspired
I can ...

Dreams/First thoughts

Reminders/Appointments

AM

PM

Brain Dump/Reminder/Notes

Today, I am grateful for ......
and I appreciate ......

Plan My Day

DATE:

This morning I feel ...

Fine

Tired   Good

Exhasuted   Fantastic

I feel this way because...

Today my top 3 priority actions are:

To feel more energized & inspired
I can ...

Dreams/First thoughts

Reminders/Appointments

AM

PM

Brain Dump/Reminder/Notes

Today, I am grateful for ......
and I appreciate ......

Plan My Day

DATE:

This morning I feel ...

Fine

Tired   Good

Exhasuted   Fantastic

I feel this way because...

Today my top 3 priority actions are:

To feel more energized & inspired
I can ...

Dreams/First thoughts

Reminders/Appointments

AM

PM

Brain Dump/Reminder/Notes

Today, I am grateful for ......
and I appreciate ......

Self-Reflection

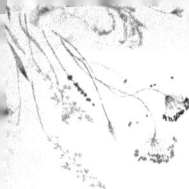

Turning It Over

My To-Do List

Universe To-Do List

Plan My Day

DATE:

This morning I feel ...

Fine

Tired   Good

Exhasuted   Fantastic

I feel this way because...

Today my top 3 priority actions are:

To feel more energized & inspired
I can ...

Dreams/First thoughts

Reminders/Appointments

AM

Brain Dump/Reminder/Notes

PM

Today, I am grateful for ......
and I appreciate ......

Plan My Day

DATE:

This morning I feel ...

Fine

Tired   Good

Exhasuted   Fantastic

I feel this way because...

To feel more energized & inspired
I can ...

Reminders/Appointments

AM

PM

Today my top 3 priority actions are:

Dreams/First thoughts

Brain Dump/Reminder/Notes

Today, I am grateful for ......
and I appreciate ......

Plan My Day

DATE:

This morning I feel ...

Fine

Tired   Good

Exhasuted   Fantastic

I feel this way because...

Today my top 3 priority actions are:

To feel more energized & inspired
I can ...

Dreams/First thoughts

Reminders/Appointments

AM

PM

Brain Dump/Reminder/Notes

Today, I am grateful for ......
and I appreciate ......

Plan My Day

DATE:

This morning I feel ...

Fine

Tired   Good

Exhasuted   Fantastic

I feel this way because...

To feel more energized & inspired
I can ...

Today my top 3 priority actions are:

Dreams/First thoughts

Reminders/Appointments

AM

PM

Brain Dump/Reminder/Notes

Today, I am grateful for ......
and I appreciate ......

Plan My Day

DATE: _____

This morning I feel ...

Fine

Tired   Good

Exhasuted   Fantastic

I feel this way because...

Today my top 3 priority actions are:

To feel more energized & inspired
I can ...

Dreams/First thoughts

Reminders/Appointments

Brain Dump/Reminder/Notes

AM

_____

_____

_____

_____

_____

PM

_____

_____

_____

_____

_____

Today, I am grateful for ......
and I appreciate ......

Plan My Day

DATE:

This morning I feel ...

Fine

Tired   Good

Exhasuted   Fantastic

I feel this way because...

Today my top 3 priority actions are:

To feel more energized & inspired
I can ...

Dreams/First thoughts

Reminders/Appointments

Brain Dump/Reminder/Notes

AM

PM

Today, I am grateful for ......
and I appreciate ......

Self-Reflection

Colouring Flowers

Plan My Day

DATE:

This morning I feel ...

Fine

Tired   Good

Exhasuted   Fantastic

I feel this way because...

Today my top 3 priority actions are:

To feel more energized & inspired
I can ...

Dreams/First thoughts

Reminders/Appointments

AM

PM

Brain Dump/Reminder/Notes

Today, I am grateful for ......
and I appreciate ......

Plan My Day

DATE:

This morning I feel ...

Fine

Tired Good

Exhasuted Fantastic

I feel this way because...

Today my top 3 priority actions are:

To feel more energized & inspired
I can ...

Dreams/First thoughts

Reminders/Appointments

AM

PM

Brain Dump/Reminder/Notes

Today, I am grateful for ......
and I appreciate ......

Plan My Day

DATE:

This morning I feel ...

Fine

Tired   Good

Exhasuted   Fantastic

I feel this way because...

Today my top 3 priority actions are:

To feel more energized & inspired
I can ...

Dreams/First thoughts

Reminders/Appointments

AM

PM

Brain Dump/Reminder/Notes

Today, I am grateful for ......
and I appreciate ......

Plan My Day

DATE:

This morning I feel ...

Fine

Tired   Good

Exhasuted   Fantastic

I feel this way because...

Today my top 3 priority actions are:

To feel more energized & inspired
I can ...

Dreams/First thoughts

Reminders/Appointments

Brain Dump/Reminder/Notes

AM

PM

Today, I am grateful for ......
and I appreciate ......

Plan My Day

DATE:

This morning I feel ...

Fine

Tired   Good

Exhasuted   Fantastic

I feel this way because...

Today my top 3 priority actions are:

To feel more energized & inspired
I can ...

Dreams/First thoughts

Reminders/Appointments

Brain Dump/Reminder/Notes

AM

PM

Today, I am grateful for ......
and I appreciate ......

Plan My Day

DATE:

This morning I feel ...

Fine

Tired   Good

Exhasuted   Fantastic

I feel this way because...

Today my top 3 priority actions are:

To feel more energized & inspired
I can ...

Dreams/First thoughts

Reminders/Appointments

AM

PM

Brain Dump/Reminder/Notes

Today, I am grateful for ......
and I appreciate ......

Self-Reflection

Complete the Maze

Plan My Day

DATE:

This morning I feel ...

Fine

Tired   Good

Exhasuted   Fantastic

I feel this way because...

Today my top 3 priority actions are:

To feel more energized & inspired
I can ...

Dreams/First thoughts

Reminders/Appointments

Brain Dump/Reminder/Notes

AM

PM

Today, I am grateful for ......
and I appreciate ......

Plan My Day

DATE:

This morning I feel ...

Fine

Tired   Good

Exhasuted   Fantastic

I feel this way because...

To feel more energized & inspired
I can ...

Reminders/Appointments

AM

PM

Today my top 3 priority actions are:

Dreams/First thoughts

Brain Dump/Reminder/Notes

Today, I am grateful for ......
and I appreciate ......

Plan My Day

DATE:

This morning I feel ...

Fine

Tired   Good

Exhasuted   Fantastic

I feel this way because...

Today my top 3 priority actions are:

To feel more energized & inspired
I can ...

Dreams/First thoughts

Reminders/Appointments

Brain Dump/Reminder/Notes

AM

PM

Today, I am grateful for ......
and I appreciate ......

Plan My Day

DATE:

This morning I feel ...

Fine

Tired   Good

Exhasuted   Fantastic

I feel this way because...

To feel more energized & inspired
I can ...

Today my top 3 priority actions are:

Dreams/First thoughts

Reminders/Appointments

AM

PM

Brain Dump/Reminder/Notes

Today, I am grateful for ......
and I appreciate ......

Plan My Day

DATE:

This morning I feel ...

Fine

Tired   Good

Exhasuted   Fantastic

I feel this way because...

Today my top 3 priority actions are:

To feel more energized & inspired
I can ...

Dreams/First thoughts

Reminders/Appointments

AM

PM

Brain Dump/Reminder/Notes

Today, I am grateful for ......
and I appreciate ......

Plan My Day

DATE:

This morning I feel ...

Fine

Tired   Good

Exhasuted   Fantastic

I feel this way because...

Today my top 3 priority actions are:

To feel more energized & inspired
I can ...

Dreams/First thoughts

Reminders/Appointments

Brain Dump/Reminder/Notes

AM

PM

Today, I am grateful for ......
and I appreciate ......

Self-Reflection

Complete the Sentences

I like...

I wish ...

I wonder ...

Plan My Day

DATE:

This morning I feel ...

Fine

Tired   Good

Exhasuted   Fantastic

I feel this way because...

Today my top 3 priority actions are:

To feel more energized & inspired
I can ...

Dreams/First thoughts

Reminders/Appointments

AM

_____

_____

_____

_____

_____

_____

PM

_____

_____

_____

_____

_____

_____

Brain Dump/Reminder/Notes

Today, I am grateful for ......
and I appreciate ......

Plan My Day

DATE:

This morning I feel ...

Fine

Tired   Good

Exhasuted   Fantastic

I feel this way because...

Today my top 3 priority actions are:

To feel more energized & inspired
I can ...

Dreams/First thoughts

Reminders/Appointments

AM

PM

Brain Dump/Reminder/Notes

Today, I am grateful for ......
and I appreciate ......

Plan My Day

DATE:

This morning I feel ...

Fine
Tired   Good
Exhasuted   Fantastic

I feel this way because...

Today my top 3 priority actions are:

To feel more energized & inspired
I can ...

Dreams/First thoughts

Reminders/Appointments

AM

PM

Brain Dump/Reminder/Notes

Today, I am grateful for ......
and I appreciate ......

Plan My Day

DATE:

This morning I feel ...

Fine

Tired   Good

Exhasuted   Fantastic

I feel this way because...

Today my top 3 priority actions are:

To feel more energized & inspired
I can ...

Dreams/First thoughts

Reminders/Appointments

AM

PM

Brain Dump/Reminder/Notes

Today, I am grateful for ......
and I appreciate ......

Plan My Day

DATE:

This morning I feel ...

Fine

Tired   Good

Exhasuted   Fantastic

I feel this way because...

Today my top 3 priority actions are:

To feel more energized & inspired
I can ...

Dreams/First thoughts

Reminders/Appointments

AM

PM

Brain Dump/Reminder/Notes

Today, I am grateful for ......
and I appreciate ......

Plan My Day

DATE:

This morning I feel ...

Fine

Tired   Good

Exhasuted   Fantastic

I feel this way because...

Today my top 3 priority actions are:

To feel more energized & inspired
I can ...

Dreams/First thoughts

Reminders/Appointments

AM

PM

Brain Dump/Reminder/Notes

Today, I am grateful for ......
and I appreciate ......

Self-Reflection

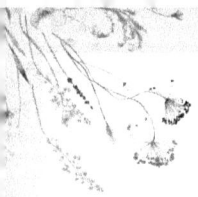

Colouring Activity

Plan My Day

DATE:

This morning I feel ...

Fine

Tired   Good

Exhasuted   Fantastic

I feel this way because...

Today my top 3 priority actions are:

To feel more energized & inspired
I can ...

Dreams/First thoughts

Reminders/Appointments

AM

PM

Brain Dump/Reminder/Notes

Today, I am grateful for ......
and I appreciate ......

Plan My Day

DATE:

This morning I feel ...

Fine

Tired   Good

Exhasuted   Fantastic

I feel this way because...

Today my top 3 priority actions are:

To feel more energized & inspired
I can ...

Dreams/First thoughts

Reminders/Appointments

Brain Dump/Reminder/Notes

AM

PM

Today, I am grateful for ......
and I appreciate ......

Plan My Day

DATE:

This morning I feel ...

Fine

Tired   Good

Exhasuted   Fantastic

I feel this way because...

Today my top 3 priority actions are:

To feel more energized & inspired
I can ...

Dreams/First thoughts

Reminders/Appointments

AM

PM

Brain Dump/Reminder/Notes

Today, I am grateful for ......
and I appreciate ......

Plan My Day

DATE:

This morning I feel ...

Fine

Tired   Good

Exhasuted   Fantastic

I feel this way because...

Today my top 3 priority actions are:

To feel more energized & inspired
I can ...

Dreams/First thoughts

Reminders/Appointments

Brain Dump/Reminder/Notes

AM

PM

Today, I am grateful for ......
and I appreciate ......

Plan My Day

DATE:

This morning I feel ...

Fine

Tired   Good

Exhasuted   Fantastic

I feel this way because...

Today my top 3 priority actions are:

To feel more energized & inspired
I can ...

Dreams/First thoughts

Reminders/Appointments

AM

PM

Brain Dump/Reminder/Notes

Today, I am grateful for ......
and I appreciate ......

Plan My Day

This morning I feel ...

Fine

Tired   Good

Exhasuted   Fantastic

I feel this way because...

Today my top 3 priority actions are:

To feel more energized & inspired
I can ...

Dreams/First thoughts

Reminders/Appointments

AM

Brain Dump/Reminder/Notes

PM

Today, I am grateful for ......
and I appreciate ......

Self-Reflection

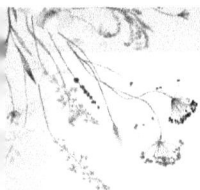

Complete the Picture

"Here Comes Trouble"

Plan My Day

DATE:

This morning I feel ...

Fine

Tired   Good

Exhasuted   Fantastic

I feel this way because...

Today my top 3 priority actions are:

To feel more energized & inspired
I can ...

Dreams/First thoughts

Reminders/Appointments

AM

PM

Brain Dump/Reminder/Notes

Today, I am grateful for ......
and I appreciate ......

Plan My Day

DATE:

This morning I feel ...

Fine

Tired   Good

Exhasuted   Fantastic

I feel this way because...

To feel more energized & inspired
I can ...

Today my top 3 priority actions are:

Dreams/First thoughts

Reminders/Appointments

AM

PM

Brain Dump/Reminder/Notes

Today, I am grateful for ......
and I appreciate ......

Plan My Day

DATE:

This morning I feel ...

Fine

Tired   Good

Exhasuted   Fantastic

I feel this way because...

Today my top 3 priority actions are:

To feel more energized & inspired
I can ...

Dreams/First thoughts

Reminders/Appointments

Brain Dump/Reminder/Notes

AM

PM

Today, I am grateful for ......
and I appreciate ......

Plan My Day

DATE:

This morning I feel ...

Fine
Tired   Good
Exhasuted   Fantastic

I feel this way because...

Today my top 3 priority actions are:

To feel more energized & inspired
I can ...

Dreams/First thoughts

Reminders/Appointments

Brain Dump/Reminder/Notes

AM

PM

Today, I am grateful for ......
and I appreciate ......

Plan My Day

DATE:

This morning I feel ...

Fine
Tired   Good
Exhasuted   Fantastic

I feel this way because...

To feel more energized & inspired
I can ...

Today my top 3 priority actions are:

Dreams/First thoughts

Reminders/Appointments

AM

PM

Brain Dump/Reminder/Notes

Today, I am grateful for ......
and I appreciate ......

Plan My Day

DATE:

This morning I feel ...

Fine
Tired   Good
Exhasuted   Fantastic

I feel this way because...

Today my top 3 priority actions are:

To feel more energized & inspired
I can ...

Dreams/First thoughts

Reminders/Appointments

AM

PM

Brain Dump/Reminder/Notes

Today, I am grateful for ......
and I appreciate ......

Self-Reflection

Complete the Sentences

Wouldn't it be nice if ...

Wouldn't it be nice if ...

Wouldn't it be nice if ...

Plan My Day

DATE:

This morning I feel ...

Fine

Tired   Good

Exhasuted   Fantastic

I feel this way because...

Today my top 3 priority actions are:

To feel more energized & inspired
I can ...

Dreams/First thoughts

Reminders/Appointments

AM

PM

Brain Dump/Reminder/Notes

Today, I am grateful for ......
and I appreciate ......

Plan My Day

DATE:

This morning I feel ...

Fine
Tired   Good
Exhasuted   Fantastic

I feel this way because...

Today my top 3 priority actions are:

To feel more energized & inspired
I can ...

Dreams/First thoughts

Reminders/Appointments

AM

PM

Brain Dump/Reminder/Notes

Today, I am grateful for ......
and I appreciate ......

Plan My Day

DATE:

This morning I feel ...

Fine
Tired   Good
Exhasuted   Fantastic

I feel this way because...

Today my top 3 priority actions are:

To feel more energized & inspired
I can ...

Dreams/First thoughts

Reminders/Appointments

Brain Dump/Reminder/Notes

AM

PM

Today, I am grateful for ......
and I appreciate ......

Plan My Day

DATE:

This morning I feel ...

Fine

Tired   Good

Exhasuted   Fantastic

I feel this way because...

Today my top 3 priority actions are:

To feel more energized & inspired
I can ...

Dreams/First thoughts

Reminders/Appointments

AM

PM

Brain Dump/Reminder/Notes

Today, I am grateful for ......
and I appreciate ......

Plan My Day

This morning I feel ...

Fine

Tired   Good

Exhasuted   Fantastic

I feel this way because...

To feel more energized & inspired
I can ...

Today my top 3 priority actions are:

Dreams/First thoughts

Reminders/Appointments

AM

_____
_____
_____
_____
_____
_____

PM

_____
_____
_____
_____
_____
_____
_____

Brain Dump/Reminder/Notes

Today, I am grateful for ......
and I appreciate ......

Plan My Day

DATE:

This morning I feel ...

Fine

Tired   Good

Exhasuted   Fantastic

I feel this way because...

To feel more energized & inspired
I can ...

Reminders/Appointments

AM

PM

Today my top 3 priority actions are:

Dreams/First thoughts

Brain Dump/Reminder/Notes

Today, I am grateful for ......
and I appreciate ......

Self-Reflection

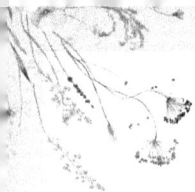

Missing Details

Complete the circles in 3 minutes, draw anything you like

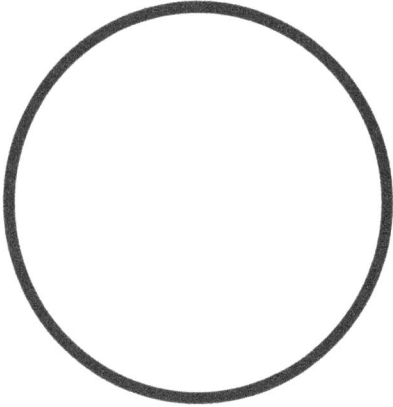

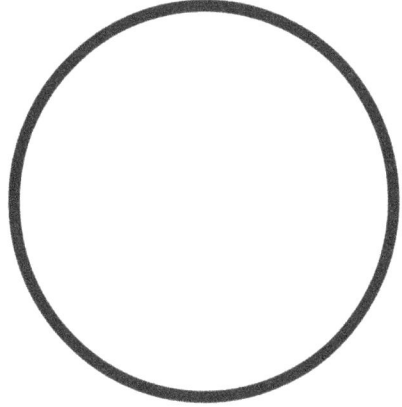

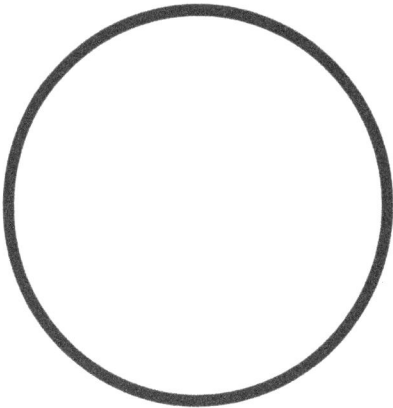

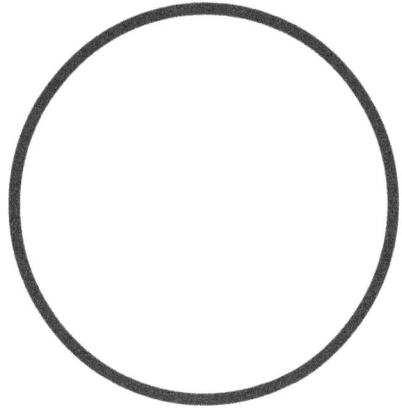

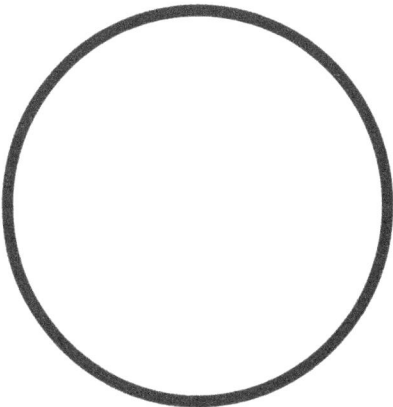

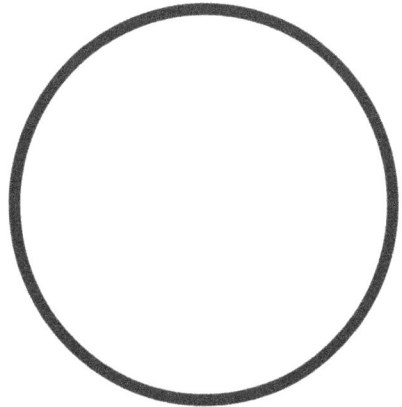

Plan My Day

DATE:

This morning I feel ...

Fine

Tired   Good

Exhasuted   Fantastic

I feel this way because...

Today my top 3 priority actions are:

To feel more energized & inspired
I can ...

Dreams/First thoughts

Reminders/Appointments

AM
_____
_____
_____
_____
_____
_____

PM
_____
_____
_____
_____
_____
_____

Brain Dump/Reminder/Notes

Today, I am grateful for ......
and I appreciate ......

Plan My Day

DATE:

This morning I feel ...

Fine

Tired   Good

Exhasuted   Fantastic

I feel this way because...

Today my top 3 priority actions are:

To feel more energized & inspired
I can ...

Dreams/First thoughts

Reminders/Appointments

Brain Dump/Reminder/Notes

AM

PM

Today, I am grateful for ......
and I appreciate ......

Plan My Day

DATE:

This morning I feel ...

Fine

Tired   Good

Exhasuted   Fantastic

I feel this way because...

Today my top 3 priority actions are:

To feel more energized & inspired
I can ...

Dreams/First thoughts

Reminders/Appointments

Brain Dump/Reminder/Notes

AM

PM

Today, I am grateful for ......
and I appreciate ......

Plan My Day

DATE:

This morning I feel ...

Fine
Tired   Good
Exhasuted   Fantastic

I feel this way because...

To feel more energized & inspired
I can ...

Today my top 3 priority actions are:

Dreams/First thoughts

Reminders/Appointments

AM

PM

Brain Dump/Reminder/Notes

Today, I am grateful for ......
and I appreciate ......

Plan My Day

DATE:

This morning I feel ...

Fine

Tired   Good

Exhasuted   Fantastic

I feel this way because...

Today my top 3 priority actions are:

To feel more energized & inspired
I can ...

Dreams/First thoughts

Reminders/Appointments

Brain Dump/Reminder/Notes

AM

PM

Today, I am grateful for ......
and I appreciate ......

Plan My Day

DATE:

This morning I feel ...

Fine

Tired   Good

Exhasuted   Fantastic

I feel this way because...

Today my top 3 priority actions are:

To feel more energized & inspired
I can ...

Dreams/First thoughts

Reminders/Appointments

AM

PM

Brain Dump/Reminder/Notes

Today, I am grateful for ......
and I appreciate ......

Self-Reflection

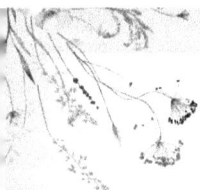

Just Doodle

Plan My Day

DATE:

This morning I feel ...

Fine
Tired   Good
Exhasuted   Fantastic

I feel this way because...

Today my top 3 priority actions are:

To feel more energized & inspired
I can ...

Dreams/First thoughts

Reminders/Appointments

AM

PM

Brain Dump/Reminder/Notes

Today, I am grateful for ......
and I appreciate ......

Plan My Day

DATE:

This morning I feel ...

Fine

Tired · Good

Exhasuted · Fantastic

I feel this way because...

Today my top 3 priority actions are:

To feel more energized & inspired
I can ...

Dreams/First thoughts

Reminders/Appointments

AM

PM

Brain Dump/Reminder/Notes

Today, I am grateful for ......
and I appreciate ......

Plan My Day

DATE:

This morning I feel ...

Fine

Tired   Good

Exhasuted   Fantastic

I feel this way because...

Today my top 3 priority actions are:

To feel more energized & inspired
I can ...

Dreams/First thoughts

Reminders/Appointments

Brain Dump/Reminder/Notes

AM

PM

Today, I am grateful for ......
and I appreciate ......

Plan My Day

DATE:

This morning I feel ...

Fine

Tired   Good

Exhasuted   Fantastic

I feel this way because...

Today my top 3 priority actions are:

To feel more energized & inspired
I can ...

Dreams/First thoughts

Reminders/Appointments

AM

PM

Brain Dump/Reminder/Notes

Today, I am grateful for ......
and I appreciate ......

Plan My Day

DATE:

This morning I feel ...

Fine

Tired   Good

Exhasuted   Fantastic

I feel this way because...

Today my top 3 priority actions are:

To feel more energized & inspired
I can ...

Dreams/First thoughts

Reminders/Appointments

AM _____

_____

_____

_____

_____

_____

PM _____

_____

_____

_____

_____

_____

Brain Dump/Reminder/Notes

Today, I am grateful for ......
and I appreciate ......

Plan My Day

DATE:

This morning I feel ...

Fine

Tired   Good

Exhasuted   Fantastic

I feel this way because...

Today my top 3 priority actions are:

To feel more energized & inspired
I can ...

Dreams/First thoughts

Reminders/Appointments

Brain Dump/Reminder/Notes

AM

PM

Today, I am grateful for ......
and I appreciate ......

Self-Reflection

Turning It Over

My To-Do List

Universe To-Do List

Plan My Day

DATE:

This morning I feel ...

Fine

Tired   Good

Exhasuted   Fantastic

I feel this way because...

Today my top 3 priority actions are:

To feel more energized & inspired
I can ...

Dreams/First thoughts

Reminders/Appointments

AM

PM

Brain Dump/Reminder/Notes

Today, I am grateful for ......
and I appreciate ......

Plan My Day

DATE:

This morning I feel ...

Fine

Tired   Good

Exhasuted   Fantastic

I feel this way because...

Today my top 3 priority actions are:

To feel more energized & inspired
I can ...

Dreams/First thoughts

Reminders/Appointments

AM

PM

Brain Dump/Reminder/Notes

Today, I am grateful for ......
and I appreciate ......

Plan My Day

DATE:

This morning I feel ...

Fine

Tired   Good

Exhasuted   Fantastic

I feel this way because...

Today my top 3 priority actions are:

To feel more energized & inspired
I can ...

Dreams/First thoughts

Reminders/Appointments

Brain Dump/Reminder/Notes

AM

PM

Today, I am grateful for ......
and I appreciate ......

Plan My Day

DATE:

This morning I feel ...

Fine

Tired   Good

Exhasuted   Fantastic

I feel this way because...

Today my top 3 priority actions are:

To feel more energized & inspired
I can ...

Dreams/First thoughts

Reminders/Appointments

AM

PM

Brain Dump/Reminder/Notes

Today, I am grateful for ......
and I appreciate ......

Plan My Day

DATE:

This morning I feel ...

Fine

Tired   Good

Exhasuted   Fantastic

I feel this way because...

Today my top 3 priority actions are:

To feel more energized & inspired
I can ...

Dreams/First thoughts

Reminders/Appointments

Brain Dump/Reminder/Notes

AM

PM

Today, I am grateful for ......
and I appreciate ......

Plan My Day

DATE:

This morning I feel ...

Fine

Tired   Good

Exhasuted   Fantastic

I feel this way because...

To feel more energized & inspired
I can ...

Reminders/Appointments

AM

PM

Today my top 3 priority actions are:

Dreams/First thoughts

Brain Dump/Reminder/Notes

Today, I am grateful for ......
and I appreciate ......

Self-Reflection

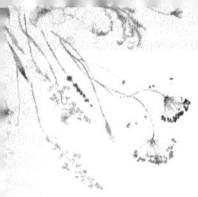

Colouring Dreamcatcher

Plan My Day

DATE:

This morning I feel ...

Fine

Tired   Good

Exhasuted   Fantastic

I feel this way because...

Today my top 3 priority actions are:

To feel more energized & inspired
I can ...

Dreams/First thoughts

Reminders/Appointments

AM

PM

Brain Dump/Reminder/Notes

Today, I am grateful for ......
and I appreciate ......

Plan My Day

DATE:

This morning I feel ...

Fine

Tired   Good

Exhasuted   Fantastic

I feel this way because...

Today my top 3 priority actions are:

To feel more energized & inspired I can ...

Dreams/First thoughts

Reminders/Appointments

AM

PM

Brain Dump/Reminder/Notes

Today, I am grateful for ......
and I appreciate ......

Plan My Day

DATE:

This morning I feel ...

Fine

Tired   Good

Exhasuted   Fantastic

I feel this way because...

Today my top 3 priority actions are:

To feel more energized & inspired
I can ...

Dreams/First thoughts

Reminders/Appointments

AM

PM

Brain Dump/Reminder/Notes

Today, I am grateful for ......
and I appreciate ......

Plan My Day

DATE:

This morning I feel ...

Fine

Tired   Good

Exhasuted   Fantastic

I feel this way because...

Today my top 3 priority actions are:

To feel more energized & inspired
I can ...

Dreams/First thoughts

Reminders/Appointments

Brain Dump/Reminder/Notes

AM

PM

Today, I am grateful for ......
and I appreciate ......

Plan My Day

DATE:

This morning I feel ...

Fine

Tired   Good

Exhasuted   Fantastic

I feel this way because...

Today my top 3 priority actions are:

To feel more energized & inspired
I can ...

Dreams/First thoughts

Reminders/Appointments

AM

_____

_____

_____

_____

_____

PM

_____

_____

_____

_____

_____

Brain Dump/Reminder/Notes

Today, I am grateful for ......
and I appreciate ......

Plan My Day

DATE:

This morning I feel ...

Fine

Tired

Good

Exhasuted

Fantastic

I feel this way because...

Today my top 3 priority actions are:

To feel more energized & inspired
I can ...

Dreams/First thoughts

Reminders/Appointments

AM

PM

Brain Dump/Reminder/Notes

Today, I am grateful for ......
and I appreciate ......

Self-Reflection

Just Doodle

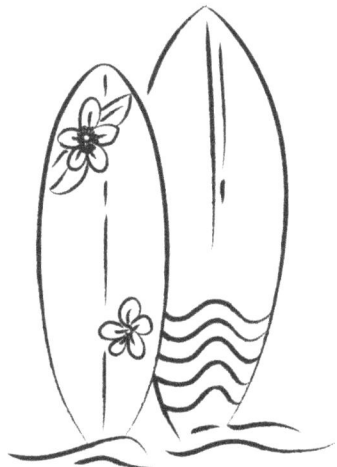

Plan My Day

DATE:

This morning I feel ...

Fine

Tired   Good

Exhasuted   Fantastic

I feel this way because...

Today my top 3 priority actions are:

To feel more energized & inspired
I can ...

Dreams/First thoughts

Reminders/Appointments

Brain Dump/Reminder/Notes

AM

PM

Today, I am grateful for ......
and I appreciate ......

Plan My Day

DATE:

This morning I feel ...

Fine

Tired   Good

Exhasuted   Fantastic

I feel this way because...

Today my top 3 priority actions are:

To feel more energized & inspired
I can ...

Dreams/First thoughts

Reminders/Appointments

Brain Dump/Reminder/Notes

AM

PM

Today, I am grateful for ......
and I appreciate ......

Plan My Day

DATE:

This morning I feel ...

Fine

Tired   Good

Exhasuted   Fantastic

I feel this way because...

Today my top 3 priority actions are:

To feel more energized & inspired
I can ...

Dreams/First thoughts

Reminders/Appointments

Brain Dump/Reminder/Notes

AM

PM

Today, I am grateful for ......
and I appreciate ......

Plan My Day

DATE:

This morning I feel ...

Fine

Tired   Good

Exhasuted   Fantastic

I feel this way because...

Today my top 3 priority actions are:

To feel more energized & inspired
I can ...

Dreams/First thoughts

Reminders/Appointments

AM

PM

Brain Dump/Reminder/Notes

Today, I am grateful for ......
and I appreciate ......

Plan My Day

DATE:

This morning I feel ...

Fine

Tired   Good

Exhasuted   Fantastic

I feel this way because...

Today my top 3 priority actions are:

To feel more energized & inspired
I can ...

Dreams/First thoughts

Reminders/Appointments

Brain Dump/Reminder/Notes

AM

PM

Today, I am grateful for ......
and I appreciate ......

Plan My Day

DATE:

This morning I feel ...

Fine

Tired   Good

Exhasuted   Fantastic

I feel this way because...

To feel more energized & inspired
I can ...

Reminders/Appointments

AM

PM

Today my top 3 priority actions are:

Dreams/First thoughts

Brain Dump/Reminder/Notes

Today, I am grateful for ......
and I appreciate ......

Self-Reflection

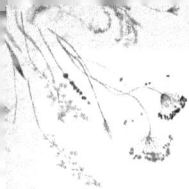

Complete the Sentences

I like...

I wish ...

I wonder ...

Plan My Day

DATE:

This morning I feel ...

Fine
Tired   Good
Exhasuted   Fantastic

I feel this way because...

Today my top 3 priority actions are:

To feel more energized & inspired
I can ...

Dreams/First thoughts

Reminders/Appointments

AM

PM

Brain Dump/Reminder/Notes

Today, I am grateful for ......
and I appreciate ......

Plan My Day

DATE:

This morning I feel ...

Fine

Tired   Good

Exhasuted   Fantastic

I feel this way because...

To feel more energized & inspired
I can ...

Reminders/Appointments

AM

PM

Today, I am grateful for ......
and I appreciate ......

Today my top 3 priority actions are:

Dreams/First thoughts

Brain Dump/Reminder/Notes

Plan My Day

DATE:

This morning I feel ...

Fine

Tired   Good

Exhasuted   Fantastic

I feel this way because...

Today my top 3 priority actions are:

To feel more energized & inspired
I can ...

Dreams/First thoughts

Reminders/Appointments

AM

PM

Brain Dump/Reminder/Notes

Today, I am grateful for ......
and I appreciate ......

Plan My Day

DATE:

This morning I feel ...

Fine

Tired   Good

Exhasuted   Fantastic

I feel this way because...

Today my top 3 priority actions are:

To feel more energized & inspired
I can ...

Dreams/First thoughts

Reminders/Appointments

AM

PM

Brain Dump/Reminder/Notes

Today, I am grateful for ......
and I appreciate ......

Plan My Day

DATE:

This morning I feel ...

Fine

Tired   Good

Exhasuted   Fantastic

I feel this way because...

Today my top 3 priority actions are:

To feel more energized & inspired
I can ...

Dreams/First thoughts

Reminders/Appointments

AM

PM

Brain Dump/Reminder/Notes

Today, I am grateful for ......
and I appreciate ......

Plan My Day

DATE:

This morning I feel ...

Fine

Tired   Good

Exhasuted   Fantastic

I feel this way because...

Today my top 3 priority actions are:

To feel more energized & inspired
I can ...

Dreams/First thoughts

Reminders/Appointments

AM

PM

Brain Dump/Reminder/Notes

Today, I am grateful for ......
and I appreciate ......

Self-Reflection

Missing Details

Complete the circles in 3 minutes, draw anything you like

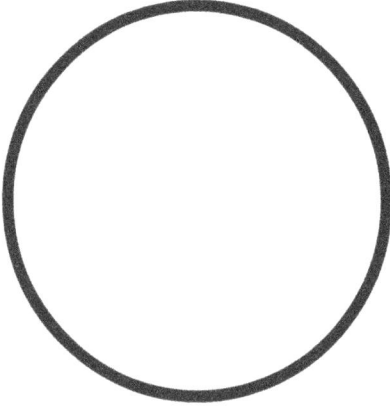

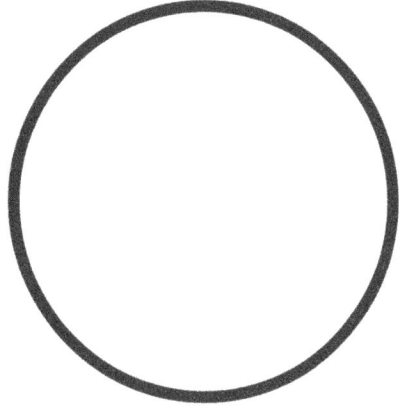

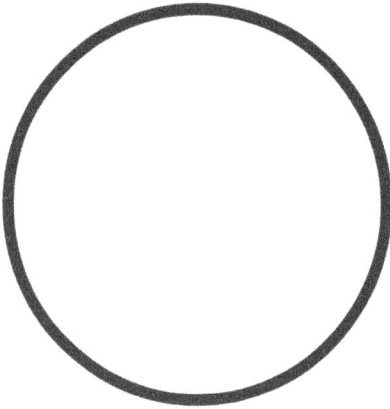

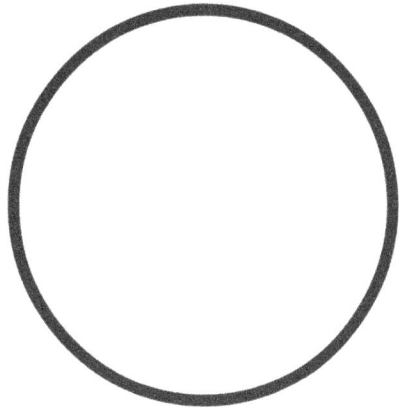

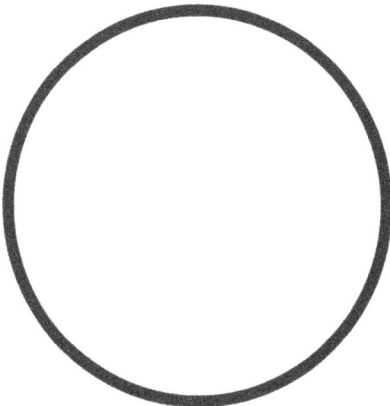

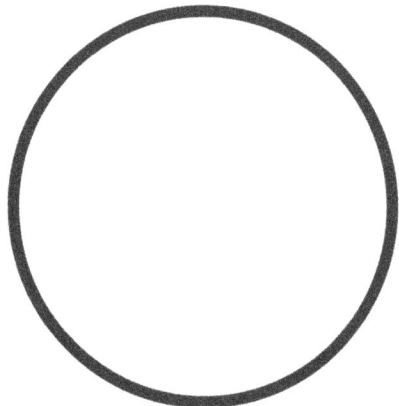

Plan My Day

DATE:

This morning I feel ...

Fine

Tired   Good

Exhasuted   Fantastic

I feel this way because...

Today my top 3 priority actions are:

To feel more energized & inspired
I can ...

Dreams/First thoughts

Reminders/Appointments

Brain Dump/Reminder/Notes

AM

PM

Today, I am grateful for ......
and I appreciate ......

Plan My Day

DATE:

This morning I feel ...

Fine

Tired   Good

Exhasuted   Fantastic

I feel this way because...

Today my top 3 priority actions are:

To feel more energized & inspired
I can ...

Dreams/First thoughts

Reminders/Appointments

AM

PM

Brain Dump/Reminder/Notes

Today, I am grateful for ......
and I appreciate ......

Plan My Day

DATE:

This morning I feel ...

Fine

Tired   Good

Exhasuted   Fantastic

I feel this way because...

Today my top 3 priority actions are:

To feel more energized & inspired
I can ...

Dreams/First thoughts

Reminders/Appointments

AM

PM

Brain Dump/Reminder/Notes

Today, I am grateful for ......
and I appreciate ......

Plan My Day

DATE:

This morning I feel ...

Fine

Tired   Good

Exhasuted   Fantastic

I feel this way because...

Today my top 3 priority actions are:

To feel more energized & inspired
I can ...

Dreams/First thoughts

Reminders/Appointments

AM

PM

Brain Dump/Reminder/Notes

Today, I am grateful for ......
and I appreciate ......

Plan My Day

DATE:

This morning I feel ...

Fine

Tired   Good

Exhasuted   Fantastic

I feel this way because...

Today my top 3 priority actions are:

To feel more energized & inspired
I can ...

Dreams/First thoughts

Reminders/Appointments

AM

PM

Brain Dump/Reminder/Notes

Today, I am grateful for ......
and I appreciate ......

Plan My Day

DATE:

This morning I feel ...

Fine

Tired   Good

Exhasuted   Fantastic

I feel this way because...

Today my top 3 priority actions are:

To feel more energized & inspired
I can ...

Dreams/First thoughts

Reminders/Appointments

AM

PM

Brain Dump/Reminder/Notes

Today, I am grateful for ......
and I appreciate ......

Self-Reflection

Colouring Mandala

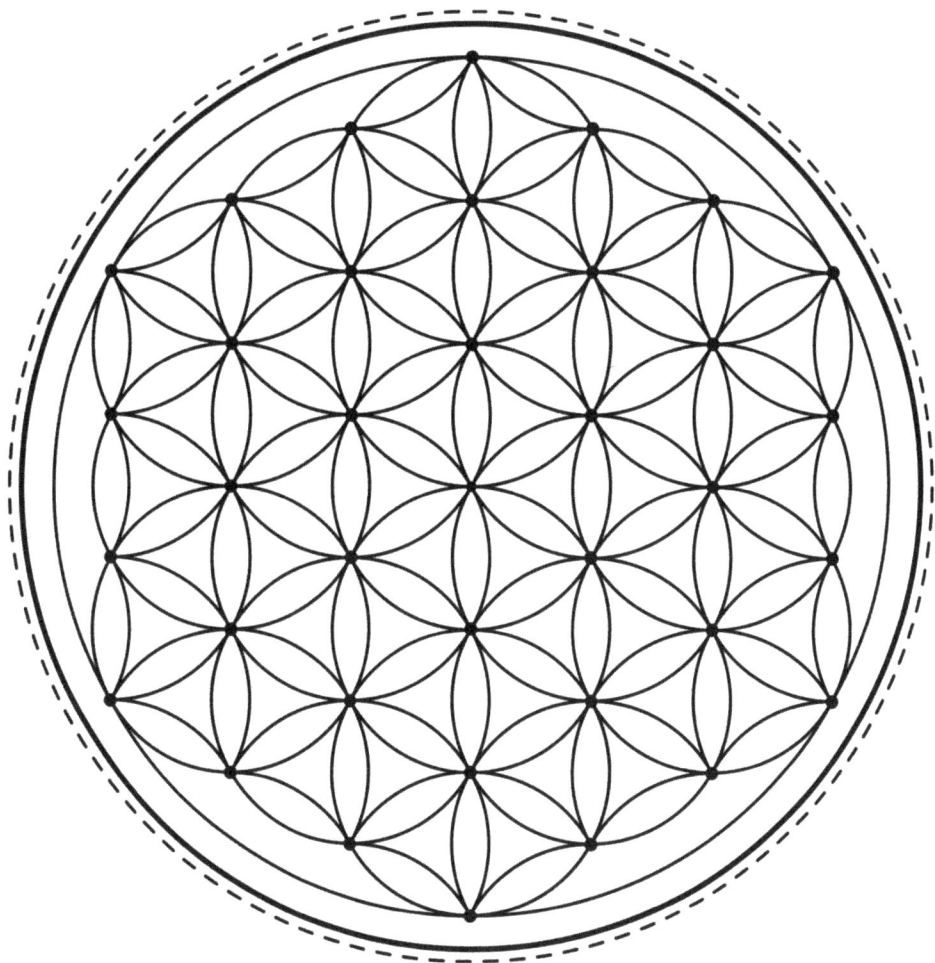

Also by Sze Wing Vetault:

Books and Planners

Goddess with Many Faces

21 Days of Inspiration

Goddess Planner 2021

Goddess Planner (Undated)

Goddess Daily Planner

For more information, please visit:
www.SzeWingVetault.com

This Goddess Daily Planner is created by Sze Wing Vetault
Copyright© 2021 by Sze Wing Vetault. All rights reserved.

About Sze Wing Vetault

Sze Wing is a coach, author and creative entrepreneur. She works with career women, busy mums and purpose-driven business owners to become goddesses in all aspects of their lives. In other words, she helps them to uncover their feminine wisdom to find better work-life balance, more joy & vitality and sustainable success in life.

With a background in Economics (BSc.) and Political Sciences (MSc.), she has built a diverse career as a business consultant for government agencies, education enterprise and film & television companies.

Sze Wing speaks, writes and promotes in the health and wellness industry. She works with other authors to publish their non-fiction books and launch creative projects. She runs a blog & podcast and she is also a mum to two beautiful young children.

She loves to do yoga, dance and travel with her family. Her favourite morning ritual includes mediation, journaling and sipping a good cup of tea!

For more information, please visit her website at
www.SzeWingVetault.com

www.ingramcontent.com/pod-product-compliance
Lightning Source LLC
Chambersburg PA
CBHW041820090426
42811CB00009B/1056